MARGO,
THANKS FOR
YOUR SUPPORT!
WILL

# Dear President Trump,

## 50 SATIRICAL LETTERS
## FROM PHOENIX TO THE WHITE HOUSE

*Insincerely,*
## WILLIAM
## FRIESE

**Dear President Trump**
Copyright © 2020 Will Friese
All rights reserved.

Published by Room 10 Publishing, LLC

ISBN: 978-1-7355700-5-1

Cover by Corey Ciszek and Corin Friese
Interior design by Amie McCracken

*To my family*
*Staci, Zoe, Emma, and Corin*
*for whom I live*


*And to my parents*
*Linda and Bill*
*who lived for me*

# TABLE OF CONTENTS

# INTRODUCTION

On November 8th, 2016, Donald J. Trump, despite losing the popular vote, won the general election to become the 45th President of the United States. The following morning, shaken, I went for an early run. I was reassured when, in about the middle of my run, the sun did indeed come up. I texted my wife, who was still at work, to let her know. She was equally distraught by the election and remained skeptical about the sunrise. She snapped, "I will confirm that myself, when I get a minute."

An absurd new world was dawning. I struggled immediately with the new administration, with its ineptitude and its tidal waves of false information. Then I read an article in the *Financial Times* and the way forward became clear. What if I stopped searching for truth in the distortion? What if I ceased objecting to wrong-footed policy? What if I gave up trying to point out the fallacies, the hypocrisy, and the shallowness?

What if I took the bait?

# US REFUGEE PROGRAM RESTRICTION

#1

1/31/17

Dear President Trump:

I wish to thank you for the recent executive order restricting the US refugee program. It seemed wise at the time, but I did not realize how much so until I read an article today in the *Financial Times*. It states that my yearly chance of being killed by a refugee in a terrorist attack is one in 3.6 billion.[1] I feel much safer now.

Mr. President, now that you have eliminated that threat, please turn your attention to vending machines. According to the article, they are about 10 times more likely to kill me than the terrorist refugees. I don't use vending machines, but sometimes I walk by them. Can you please deport these killers —perhaps to our enemies? Mexico comes to mind. If you can't deport them, then just put a wall around them. I know this program would be outrageously expensive; I am sure you can get the vending machine companies to pay for it.

Lastly, let us not ignore the elephant in the room: lightning. It is almost 100 times more likely to kill me than a terrorist refugee. Something must be done. I think we can do without this awesome display of nature, considering

---

1   Lauren Leatherby, "Trump Clampdown: Four Charts on the US Refugee Program," Financial Times, January 27, 2017, ft.com.

how dangerous it is. Can you and Kellyanne Conway create Alternative Weather that does not have lightning? I understand that alternative realities are difficult to construct. It seemed to consume your first few days in office. I know 'alternative facts' are difficult to comprehend. Even Chuck Todd, who I think is very smart, in an interview with Ms. Conway, did not seem to understand. I know you can do it. Even if I do see a lightning strike, I am sure your administration can convince me I have not. Then I will feel even safer.

Sincerely,
Will Friese
Phoenix

# HEALTHCARE

#2

3/25/17

Dear President Trump:

The American Health Care Act failed, and you blamed the Democrats. How right you are! I remember this type of thinking from when my children were young. When something goes awry, blame someone you don't like. Alas, my children grew out of this type of thinking. I'm so glad the Office of the President now embraces it.

Let us list the elements of the Democrats' culpability:

1) Laziness. Sadly, not everyone is a Republican. Republicans only have a majority in the Senate and the House, and no concerns about a veto from the presidency. But they can't do it alone, obviously. Lazy Democrats need to do their fair share.

2) Ungratefulness. Republicans saved the Democrats all the hassle of drafting legislation by not consulting them—they even served that favor upon some of their own. It seems reasonable that Democrats could return the favor and rubber-stamp the Act.

3) Jealousy. Who knew healthcare was so complex? Who knew the Republicans would master it so quickly? They turned out a bill so elegant that almost all interested parties opposed it, not to mention 83% of the public.

Jealousy of the Republican legislative and political prowess kept Democrats on the sidelines.

4) Spite. I know Obamacare was probably Obama's and the Democrats' greatest accomplishment, but why are they so defensive? I guess all those votes to repeal without any replacement put them on edge. Now they just want Republicans to fail.

But Republicans came up with a bill and quickly. The Republicans are in charge now, and Democrats should follow their lead and vote with them. Give the Hangman some rope. Give the Arsonist some matches. Let's all hop on the Trump Train to oblivion. What could go wrong ... except 24 million more uninsured Americans.

Sincerely,
Will Friese
Phoenix

# FIDGET SPINNER

**#3**

5/10/17

Dear President Trump:

Using Hillary Clinton's email investigation as an excuse for firing FBI Director Comey is simply brilliant. No one will know the real reason: that you are too insecure to tolerate an investigation into your campaign's relationship with Russia. I love the part where you state that Comey has told you on three separate occasions that you are *not* being investigated. No one will see your ulterior motive.

Next time, though, if you want to stay out of the public eye, just send in the secret weapon you employed at the Korean demilitarized zone: Mike Pence. Have him scowl at your detractor, just like he did at all of North Korea. That surely would have cowed Comey into dropping the Russia investigation. Don't forget to dress up Vice President Pence in the bomber jacket—a great effect! I still get shivers thinking of those photos.

But alas, my President, I write to give you a little advice. Some of your misstatements and lies, not as well-crafted as Comey-Clinton lie above, are coming to light, and I think they may have a cumulative effect on your public support. You said that your proposed American Health Care Act protects people with preexisting conditions, that you mandated it—but we know it does not. China is a currency manipulator; it is not, and now you agree. Andrew Jackson was angry about the Civil War. That's a bad one. Everyone knows Jackson loved war. You once said that your sister, a judge, signs legislation into law. Is that something you recently mandated? I learned something different in sixth grade. The inauguration attendance, voter fraud, Obama wiretapping, bad Muslims, bad Mexicans, locker room talk …

I am concerned that you are unengaged or incompetent, or possibly both. Your presidency would be laughable if one could laugh at the downfall of something so important. I want to help. As you said, this job is a lot harder than you thought it would be. But you can do it. You just need a little help focusing. I suggest you buy a fidget spinner. It is a small toy to help you concentrate. Use it, get your focus back, and then address the nation's pressing problems.

Sincerely,
Will Friese
Phoenix

# PARIS CLIMATE ACCORD

## 4

6/3/17

Dear President Trump:

This is my fourth letter to you, and I need to say, I have a day job. So, to quote Mitch McConnell, "we could do with a little less drama from the White House." But what drama it was from the Rose Garden. You rightfully withdrew from the Paris Accord. I loved the halting prose you used to deliver the news. It was like a second grader reading a book report, but a little slower. You showed those other countries—pretty much *all* the other countries. They were laughing at us, you said, for planning to reduce our carbon emissions by 27% over 20 years. That seems totally impractical, given all the new clean energy technology that is being developed here in the States. Now they are certainly going to stop laughing as the world's historically largest carbon polluter turns its back on emissions reductions.

We are now in a special group of countries that reject the Paris Accord: The United States, Syria, and Nicaragua. What a trio! Except Nicaragua does not belong; they actually wanted tougher requirements. So it's just Syria and us. Syria has a strong leader, just like you. Maybe we should do more stuff like Syria. Are things working out for the Syrians?

You really showed those Europeans that we will not be bullied, even though in the Paris Accord, we set our own emissions standards. But that is beside the point. We, as you said, have reasserted "America's Sovereignty." You are such a smart man. I did not even know we lost our sovereignty. I am delighted to have it back.

I most loved the way you manhandled reality and science and twisted it into something completely unrecognizable. Those dopes at MIT had the audacity to say you misused their studies. Who cares about MIT? Scott Pruitt, our EPA director, says there are other studies that state the Paris Accord is useless. He is so good at protecting the environment.

As a former resident of Pittsburgh, I was proud when you said, "I was elected to represent the citizens of Pittsburgh, not Paris." I know you care about Pittsburgh a lot more than the coastal cities, which will flood as the world warms. To hell with New York and Miami. They didn't vote for you. Actually, neither did Pittsburgh. I think only 25% of Pittsburgh "elected" you. Alas, I'm sure they are all behind you now, just like the Mayor of Pittsburgh. When he heard your Pittsburgh reference, I think he said he "loved" it, or maybe he was "livid." I get those two words mixed up. Just like you mixed up the old steel town, Pittsburgh of the 1940s, and the forward-looking, Paris Accord-embracing, Pittsburgh of 2017.

You should visit Pittsburgh. At least learn a little about it before you throw its good name around in an announcement a majority of the citizens disagree with. It's a beautiful, vibrant, and friendly city that has transformed itself after the downfall of the steel industry. And while you are there, maybe the good people can also teach you a little bit about alliteration. Pittsburgh and Paris...Pathetic.


Sincerely,
Will Friese
Phoenix

# PORTLAND

## #5

6/6/17

Dear President Trump:

When I submitted my last letter, I noticed that the White House website only permits 2500 characters. That seems arbitrary since everyone knows your attention span is limited to 140 characters. I'll keep this short. Are you still reading?

I have been very supportive of you in the past. However, I need to take issue with your response to the recent tragedy in Portland. A white man shouted anti-Muslim insults at two teenage girls and then stabbed three men that rose in the girls' defense. Ricky Best and Taliesin Namkai-Meche died; Micah Fletcher survived.

Your response three days later, via tweet from @Potus: "The violent attacks in Portland on Friday are unacceptable. The victims were standing up to hate and intolerance. Our prayers are w/them."

Your response is inadequate. It is shamefully bereft of substance and scope. "Unacceptable" is the position you take when your child gets a C in math, not when people are senselessly and brutally murdered. Your thoughtless choice of words pales against your failure to identify the real issue. This was an act of hate fueled by Islamophobia, which you have personally fostered.

Edmund Burke said, "The only thing necessary for the triumph of evil is for good men to do nothing." Are you a good man like Ricky Best? Are you a good man like Taliesin Namkai-Meche? Are you a good man like Micah Fletcher? They stood up to "hate and intolerance." Why don't you?

Sincerely,
Will Friese
Phoenix

# ERIC

6/7/17

Dear President Trump:

I am sorry to bother you again, but I had to write. I just saw your son Eric interviewed by Sean Hannity. You must be so proud. The more I get to know him, the more he reminds of you! He cited the imploding Democratic Party. That is extraordinarily insightful, since there actually is no outward sign of such implosion. It reminds me of when you described *The New York Times* as failing. That's too bad. They are such a great source of news. I quickly bought a subscription after you said that. I hope it helped them.

I liked the part where Eric blamed the Democrats for obstructing your agenda. That is a classic Trump obfuscation. We know who is primarily responsible for derailing your agenda. Hint: his first name starts with a "D" and he tweets a lot.

Eric complained that he has never seen so much hate. I don't understand it either. You have belittled our allies, weakened NATO (which has promoted unprecedented peace), pulled out of the Trans-Pacific Partnership (which took years to negotiate), threatened NAFTA, demeaned the judiciary, and insulted our neighbors. The administration wants to defund Planned Parenthood, resume mandatory sentencing for nonviolent crimes, decrease spending for education and our national parks, ban Muslims, cut access to healthcare, and cut taxes for the rich ... I could go on, but I don't see much to hate.

The best line of the interview was when Eric said that Democrats are "not even people." That sure resonates with me. About half the time after I really get to know someone, even when we have a lot of common interests, I find out that they're a Democrat. Then I think, wow, you're not really a person, and you're probably filled with hate. It's funny that the root of Democrat, demos, means "people." That's awfully misleading.

I'm glad Eric is speaking out more. It's reassuring to know that there is another Trump just like you. It gives me great comfort to know that in eight years, there will be someone ready to replace you.


Sincerely,
Will Friese
Phoenix

# CHARLOTTESVILLE

*#7*

8/16/17

Dear President Trump:

Boy, that infrastructure-turned-Charlottesville press conference Tuesday was a doozy. You were widely criticized. The failing *New York Times* reported that you felt liberated after the conference. If I had all that crazy stuff rolling around in my head, I would feel liberated too after spewing it out everywhere. I noticed your chief of staff kept his head down the whole time; probably didn't want to get any of it on his face.

Let's review the crazy you let out:

1) Comparing George Washington to Robert E. Lee. Only a skilled orator like you could pull this off. One man singularly kept the Constitutional Convention together that founded our republic and the other literally tried to break it in half. They do both have white hair ...

2) Alt-Left invention. Great idea. I hope it is hate-based like the Alt-Right. That would be a nice symmetry.

3) Blaming John McCain for the failure of the substance-less healthcare bill. I love it when you look to others for your shortfalls.

4) Blaming both sides in Charlottesville, the racist side and the anti-racist side. It takes two to tango! If the left stayed home, there would not have been a problem... except for the rampant racism.

5) You said, "I am not putting anyone on a moral plane." That's for presidents past. Principle and ethics do not guide you; only the appearance of winning matters.

Getting all that crazy out was a very healthy and necessary step. It's similar to when you tweeted that transgender individuals will no longer serve in the military. That is one of the craziest things yet. How about that cartoon you retweeted with the Trump Train running over a fake news CNN person? Sadly, it reminded me of the car driving into the Charlottesville protesters that killed Heather Heyer. It was good you took it down 20 minutes later. I will never forget what Ms. Heyer said: "If you're not outraged, you're not paying attention."

So with all that crazy stuff out of your head, you can get back to work on infrastructure, tax reform, and kicking sand in Kim Jong-un's face. Things may be a little bit harder, as some of your support is fading. I liked how you fired your two business advisory councils right after they decided to quit. It is so respectful to break up by tweet or email. It saves the other person in the relationship a lot of time and angst that a face-to-face meeting would entail. Also, your military is being uncharacteristically outspoken. I hope you can still count on them.

Regardless of how many people around you clamor for the exit, I know you will get right back to making

America great again. And none too soon, a lot of damage has been done since January 20th.


Sincerely,
Will Friese
Phoenix

P.S. See you at the Phoenix Convention Center next Tuesday!

# ARPAIO

# 8

8/26/17

Dear President Trump:

I am so glad you pardoned Sheriff Joe Arpaio. All he did
was disobey a court order and cost taxpayers millions in
legal fees. "So, was Sheriff Joe convicted for doing his
job?" you asked at your rally in Phoenix last Tuesday. If
racial profiling and detaining people illegally was part
of his job, hell yes, he was doing his job! Was he also
violating the Constitution? Hell yes, again! I see why
you came down on the side of a man trying to do his job
instead of that cumbersome document that our country
was founded upon. Did you willfully disregard your
inaugural oath? You probably just forgot it. Here is a
refresher: "I will faithfully execute the Office of President of the United States, and will to the best of my
ability, preserve, protect and defend the Constitution of
the United States."

What is the big deal with racial profiling anyway? I do
it all the time. For instance, whenever I see a white
person with a comb-over, I think, "insecure idiot," and
I am usually right. The people of Phoenix are squarely
behind you. It was smart not to announce the pardon
at your rally. The resulting celebration and jubilation
would have been difficult for the police to manage. It
was wise to make that declaration while you were squir-

reled away back in Washington DC. Some say you were afraid to do it here; however, I know what a brave man it takes to do the right thing and go against the Constitution and our justice system.

Sadly, I lost my ticket to your rally, and I was forced to hang around outside with the protestors. I was surprised to see so many people. I'm still not sure why they were protesting, but they had some very interesting signs:

Im-Peach the Orange
Hands Too Small to Build a Wall
The Alt-Right is All-Wrong
Super-Callous-Fragile-Racist-Sexist-Nazi-POTUS
Mr. Hate, Leave our State
Dump Trump
Not my President
Not my Cheeto
Refugees Welcome
You Can't Comb Over Hate
Control, Alt-Right, Delete
Hate has no Home Here
Love Trumps Hate
Stop Pretending Your Racism is Patriotism
Trump is a Yuge Mistake
No Hate in 48

In case you forgot, Arizona was the 48th state admitted to the union. Perhaps it will be the first to leave, based on the tenor of these signs. Just kidding—most of us think you're doing a great job. Given how well you are doing, these signs sure showed a lot of imagination. I do wish you would show a little more imagination in office.

Instead of trying to build on past successes, you focus on undoing past legislation—with particular attention to the Obama administration. I often get a funny image. Obama and his administrators are children on the beach building sandcastles. One castle is Obamacare, another is Clean Energy, another is National Monuments, etc. ... Then you come walking along the beach, a big, tall, tough president, and kick over all the sandcastles. Funny! Right?! Pardoning Arpaio is like kicking over a Justice sandcastle. Except that castle was created by the Constitution. I recommend you stop being so destructive and use your imagination to build more. I know you have a great imagination. Few people are creative enough to imagine "fine" people on the side of the Nazis and the KKK.

Sincerely,
Will Friese
Phoenix

# ECLIPSE

9/4/17

Dear President Trump:

I love that picture of you looking at the eclipse without any protective eyewear. You ignored the advice given to school children and the population ad-nauseam: don't look directly at the sun, it's bad for your eyes. But you showed your superiority. You didn't go blind. You don't need to listen.

Nothing matters except what you think matters... dissenters be damned!

Damn the economists that espouse the benefits of free trade.
Damn the scientists that have demonstrated the reality of climate change.
Damn the healthcare industry that was opposed to your Obamacare repeal.
Damn the social scientists that show the necessity and benefit of immigration.
Damn the journalists and their fake news.
Damn the truth when it does not suit you!
Damn the dissenters. You don't need them. You don't need anyone.

It reminds me of another picture. You are at your desk in the oval office, surrounded by Mike Pence, Sean Spicer,

Steve Bannon, Michael Flynn and Reince Priebus. The latter four are gone. Do you still need Pence? I guess you should be careful. The more people you push away, the fewer will be around when you really need someone.

Sincerely,
Will Friese
Phoenix

# THE CAMBODIA DAILY

9/5/17

Dear President Trump:

Congratulations are in order! *The Cambodia Daily*, an independent newspaper located in Phnom Penh, Cambodia, has closed. They were issued a $6.3 million back tax bill by their increasingly authoritarian government looking to crack down on free speech. You can give yourself a small pat on the back for a job well done. As your administration belittles domestic journalistic institutions, foreign powers are emboldened to make real limitations on free speech.

In February, Phay Siphan, a Cambodian government spokesman, stated—in reference to CNN and *The New York Times* being excluded from a press conference—that "President Donald Trump thinks that the news reported by these organizations did not reflect the truth, which is the responsibility of the professional reporters." The spokesman continued: "This means that freedom of expression must respect the law and the authority of the state."

I agree that *The New York Times* and CNN should not be contradicting you with things like facts. You are the president. They didn't win the election. I think free speech is important, but they should show some respect and stop saying things that you disagree with.

Some say free speech is the lynchpin of democracy. I guess you would like to find out.


Sincerely,
Will Friese
Phoenix

## DOTARD

9/22/17

Dear President Trump:

I just read that Kim Jong-un of North Korea called you a "mentally deranged U.S. dotard." I thought "dotard" must be Korean for "strong president that should be feared and respected." Boy, was I wrong. I looked it up. Dotard is an English word. Can you believe that Rocket Man knows an English word that most Americans don't know? For the record, a dotard is someone in his dotage. According to Merriam-Webster, a dotage is, "a state or period of senile decay marked by decline of mental poise and alertness."

I have to say, Kim Jong-un ... nailed it!! You are totally a dotard! But who cares? We (your unwavering supporters) have always known you're crazy. Case in point, not just two days ago, speaking at the UN you said the U.S. would completely destroy North Korea. Is it not well known that the U.S. has that capability? Does the 150-pound schoolyard bully need to constantly inform the 50-pound kids they should not physically attack him? Could these unnecessary statements be misinterpreted as threats, prevent diplomacy, or even provoke a preemptive strike?

Here's another crazy thing—a crazy irony. You threatened

the existence of another nation at the United Nations. The UN is an organization devoted to maintaining international peace and security through cooperation. It's no wonder John Kelly covered his face during your speech. Press Secretary Sarah Huckabee Sanders said he was tired. Tired all right—tired of your crazy talk.

But John Kelly is not one of your true supporters like me. I know you know what is best. North Korea needs to shut up and stop shooting their missiles everywhere. America needs to win this fight! Winning is all that matters! So what if we wipe out 50 million North Koreans – are they not asking for it? Don't they hate us anyway? So what if, in the process, North Korea kills 10 million South Koreans in Seoul and another 20 million Japanese in Tokyo? The North Korean threat will then be eliminated.

Admittedly, North Korea might get off an ICBM aimed at the U.S. mainland. But we can shoot those down. Our anti-missile defenses work at least 50% of the time. I am willing to roll those dice. I know you are. Once this North Korean thing is wrapped up, you can focus on tax reform.

I discussed this with a friend, and he said destroying North Korea would be a pyrrhic victory. I already looked up one definition today. Can you look up "pyrrhic" and get back to me?


Sincerely,
Will Friese
Phoenix

# THE NFL

#12

9/24/17

Dear President Trump:

I know you are busy today creating problems where they don't exist. Only a great president could offend the NFL and the NBA and still have time to threaten Kim Jong-un. Make me proud and figure out a way to insult the Chicago Cubs and NASCAR while maintaining the nuclear brinkmanship.

I think it's important that you know about something that's going on right now in your White House. As you well know, I have been very busy writing you supportive letters. After I do, I usually receive this email from the Office of Presidential Correspondence:

"Thank you for contacting the White House. We are carefully reviewing your message."

You go on to say that you, President Donald J. Trump, believe "the strength of our country lies in the spirit of the American people and their willingness to stay informed and get involved," and that you are appreciative of me "taking the time to reach out."

So, I have a question for the Office of Presidential Correspondence, given their statement that you like the American people to be spirited and involved: do they *know* you? For example, NFL players kneeling during the National Anthem and NBA players considering not accepting an invitation to the White House **are** informed and **are** getting involved. Yet, you just said the NFL players should be fired and the NBA players uninvited. Quite a contrast from the Office of Presidential Correspondence. Rightly so! I agree with you. People should stay dumb and mind their own business. Respect the flag, respect the President, and shut-up!

I did find someone that disagrees with us: Thomas Jefferson. I know you like him because you are an ardent defender of his statues. He wrote, "it is their right, it is their duty, to throw off such Government, and to provide new Guards." This is, of course, from the Declaration of Independence—the greatest document ever written—and refers to the colonists rising up against British rule. It has always struck me that disobedience to unfair government is not merely a right; it is a *duty*.

But obviously, kneeling at the National Anthem or refusing to visit the White House goes way too far. You need to talk to the Office of Presidential Correspondence and have them change the email reply. I have a suggestion below:

*The White House*

*Washington, DC*

*Thank you for contacting the White House. We are carefully reviewing your message.*

*President Donald J. Trump is insecure and really does not like it when people disagree with him. If your message contains even a hint of negativity or disagreement, it will be trashed. If you completely agree with the President and gush about the President in a way that makes us throw up in our mouths a little, then we may forward your message. Don't hold your breath, but keep the support coming. President Trump appreciates you taking the time to reach out.*

*If you wish to receive regular email updates from the White House, please Click Here. You may also wish to follow President Trump and the White House on Facebook, Instagram, Twitter, and YouTube.*

*Sincerely,*

*The Office of Presidential Correspondence*

You are welcome in advance.

Sincerely,
Will Friese
Phoenix

# TAX CUT

**#13**

12/24/17

Dear President Trump:

Merry Christmas and thanks for the tax cut. It was nice the way you got all those "fiscal hawks" like Senators Jeff Flake and Bob Corker to roll over for political expediency. I hope the Republican donors got a nice tax cut too. They earned it.

I understand the tax cut will cause the United States to incur another 1 trillion dollars of debt over the next 10 years.[2] No worries, our kids* are smart, they will figure out how to pay back our irresponsible spending. I know what you are saying: the cut will pay for itself by stimulating the economy. Wink, wink. You are such a card! Ha Ha Ha! You know very well nobody believes that. Why should we? Trickle-down economics has never worked before.

You are such a great president; you gave us a Christmas tax cut *and* something to laugh about.

Sincerely,
Will Friese
Phoenix

---

2   Joint Committee on Taxation. "Macroeconomic Analysis of the "Tax Cut and Jobs Act" as Ordered Reported by the Senate Committee on Finance on November 16, 2017.

\* The term "our kids" refers to America's children and not specifically to *your* children, for whom the adjective "smart" does not typically come to mind.

# CDC

## 14

12/25/17

Dear President Trump:

Congratulations are in order! I love your new technique for obscuring the truth. Typically, you just lie. And you do it so brilliantly—like no other president ever. I am sure you fool most of us. *The New York Times* says that since you came into office, you tell about 10 lies a month. You should be proud. You are much better at lying than President Obama. He only lied about twice per year. Amateur!

But you have moved on from the straightforward lie. Your administration told the Center for Disease Control that there were seven words or phrases they could not use: "diversity," "entitlement," "fetus," "transgender," "vulnerable," "evidence-based" and "science-based." This is a cutting-edge, dictator-style form of administration. George Orwell would exalt you (he wrote *1984*, it's a book ... never mind). The CDC is a science-based organization and you just tied their hands. I am sure the CDC will just stop doing science now and start making shit up. That will be easier than complicated research and will certainly save money. Our country will be better off.

What does the CDC really do anyway? From the CDC website: "The CDC works 24/7 to protect America from health, safety, and security threats, both foreign and in the U.S.," blah, blah, blah. There is more, but sounds like a lot of wasted taxpayer money. Maybe you can get my doctor to stop using evidence-based medicine and I will not have to wait so long in his waiting room.

You should continue this policy with the FBI. Tell them that they can no longer use the word "investigation." Without "Investigation," they will just be another "Federal Bureau." The good Lord knows we have enough of those, and you can just shutter it. That will teach them for *not* investigating Hillary enough and you too much.

Let's not stop there. How about the Environmental Protection Agency? That's another agency you could care less about. You put Scott Pruitt in charge; as Attorney General of Oklahoma, he had sued the EPA. I wonder who is going to win that lawsuit? Instead of censoring certain words, don't let those geeks at the EPA use any words at all, only numbers. They can just stay in their labs and figure stuff out but not talk to anyone about it. Then they will not get in the way of business and we can have some real economic growth, just like China.

Of course we might get the air and water quality of China also. According to the Chinese Ministry of Health, half the population is without clean water and hundreds of thousands die annually from air pollution. You might need to change your motto to "Make America Great Again, Wear a Mask, and Drink Bottled Water." But that will not fit on your red hat. Maybe "Make America Great

Again at Any Cost." That would fit, but there would need to be an asterisk next to "Great." Some would argue that if we sacrifice clean air and water for economic growth, are we really "great" or just big and dirty? I think we can agree upon "Make America Big and Dirty" as representative but also economical enough to fit on a hat.

Oh what havoc you can wreak when you censor what people can say. I guess that's why we have the First Amendment. Funny it does not apply to the CDC. Or does it? Maybe you should get rid of the First Amendment too!

Merry Christmas and Happy Censoring,
Will Friese
Phoenix

# SHITHOLE

# #15

1/15/18

Dear President Trump:

Thank you for describing African nations and Haiti as "shithole countries." Not because it's true; it's not. Not because it clearly shows you're racist; it does not. Besides, we already know that you're a racist.

I thank you because now we get to use another profanity without consequence. You remember when "pussy" was off limits for regular conversation? Not after the Access Hollywood tape. I say pussy all the time now. It's no big deal. Your "locker room talk" made "pussy" fair game – just like a woman's genitalia.

Now, after your "Oval Office talk," we have "shithole." I can't wait to start using this in formal settings, just like my president. I talked to my kids about this. If it's acceptable for the Oval Office, it's acceptable for the dinner table. My children would like some other words cleared for daily conversation: asshat, wangjangalow, and dickweed. Perhaps you can work one or two of those into the State of the Union address. I will be listening. I can't wait to find out if America is great again!

Sincerely,
Will Friese
Phoenix

# STORMY DANIELS

#16

5/6/18

Dear President Trump:

I wish to extend my sincere thanks and gratitude to you for introducing me to Stormy Daniels. I had never heard of her...or Madison Young or Nina Hartley or Christy Canyon or Stoya or any other adult film actresses, because, of course, I don't watch porn. I have many preconceptions about porn stars and was surprised by Ms. Daniels' character. She is well spoken and obviously quite intelligent. She is savvy and restrained. I see why you liked her; opposites attract.

Perhaps you also liked her because she can do something you have never been able to do: speak the truth. I think you and your administration could learn a thing or two from her. But, alas, why start with the truth now. Lying is what got you here. But where are we? There is no wall, no NAFTA renegotiation, no Obamacare repeal, coal mining is still in retreat, the middle class and poor have received no relief—except for the tax cut, wink, wink—and Hillary is free.

My dear President, you are a liar par excellence. The *Washington Post* said you told your 3000th lie in office. However, you need to step up your game. The truth is coming: Stormy Daniels, Mueller, the midterm elections. We are going to need some Trump-sized lies to overcome all of these facts. Don't be bashful. You don't need to worry about accountability. My head is firmly up my ass, like the rest of your base.

Sincerely,
Will Friese
Phoenix

# RED FOR ED

**#17**

5/13/18

Dear President Trump:

Nice job backing out of the Iran Deal. I can't wait to see the fallout from that – did you get the pun? Probably not, let's move on. I need to interrupt your tirade against the Obama legacy and tell you about something terrible in Arizona: "Red for Ed." First of all, they stole your color. Red is for hats that are making America great again. Red is not for education. That must be a form of treason. Have your friend Attorney General Jeff Sessions look into it when he's not too busy criminalizing marijuana and keeping nonviolent criminals locked up.

Secondly, they are trying to ruin your tax cuts. I recently heard you say we are *all* doing fine because of your tax cuts. I guess the teachers in Arizona didn't get the message. They are demanding things that are going to make our state taxes go up and cancel the benefits of your federal cut. They want spending on education returned to 2008 levels, before the great recession. They complain that the average spending in Arizona per pupil is $7,500 whereas the national average $11,400. That is 34% lower. The Arizona median teacher salary is $46,900 compared to $56,300 for the national average. That is 17% lower. Arizona currently spends $924 *less* per student than it did in 2008. The teachers don't just want more money for themselves; they want it for the whole system. They argue that our country thrives when everyone thrives, since today's children will be paying our Social Security and Medicare benefits. They claim education is the great equalizer and provides opportunity where there is little—I guess not everyone gets a million dollars from his dad. Teachers say that education provides opportunities to our brightest to pursue the American dream. The resultant increase in productivity benefits all. It is anti-American to under-fund public education.

That's all well and good, as long as my taxes don't go up. So get down here and work your magic; convince Arizonans that lower taxes—especially for the wealthy—are more important than a solid public education for all. Sprinkle some of that trickle down bullshit over the greater Phoenix area. Governor Ducey is under a lot of pressure. He can't use that common Congressional tactic where you increase spending and cut taxes—while the deficit quietly increases and the national debt accelerates. Arizona cannot print money and we have to balance the budget. Our teachers are just getting started and already have a lot of public support. They will be back at it in the fall. Something is going to pop; I fear it will be my taxes. Help!

Sincerely,
Will Friese
Phoenix

cc: Governor Doug Ducey

## 18

# BE BEST

5/16/18

Dear President Trump:

You should be very proud of the First Lady and her "Be Best" Campaign. I like the part where she comes out against cyberbullying. It made me think about what a bully is. A bully is someone that uses power to intimidate or influence someone weaker. Usually the bully has some insecurity. The bully will not be bothered with facts or fairness; he just wants to get his way. Remind you of anyone? That's right, it's a perfect description of the 45th President of the United States, Donald Trump, "The Bully in Chief." After being married to you for 13 years, it's no surprise she chose anti-bullying as a topic to promote.

One of the main Be Best materials, for which she claimed co-authorship, was actually created by the Federal Trade Commission during the Obama administration. When the media pointed this out, they were admonished in a statement from her office. You know what that sounds like? Yep...bullying. The irony is thick. Is she a bully too? If so, she is off to a good start. There's no doubt where she learned it. Pat yourself on the back and the First Lady wherever you feel it is appropriate.

Sincerely,
Will Friese
Phoenix

## 19

# SINGAPORE NOBEL

5/20/18

Dear President Trump:

Finally, the world community now recognizes what an excellent negotiator you are and will soon give you the Nobel Peace Prize for your work on the Korean Peninsula. You deserve the prize because nobody negotiates peace like you. For example, pulling out of the Iran deal was a brilliant move. Iran was at least seven years away from developing a nuclear weapon, and now they can do it right away! That sends a clear message that you don't think logically, and therefore, no one can predict your next move. You said it yourself: even *you* don't know what you are going to do next. You really throw people off when you tell the truth. Some say you're being coy, but I believe you. You haven't a clue. This is a huge advantage during negotiations. They can't outfox you if they can't predict what you're thinking. Let them try. We know there is nothing going on up there.

Another example of your paradigm-breaking thinking: threatening nuclear holocaust as a way to get North Korea to the negotiating table. It's almost like you don't know how nuclear détente works. Quick primer: you destroy us, we destroy you. I loved it when, after North Korea said they might withdraw from the summit in Singapore, you threatened them with decimation … or wealth and security if they showed up. You are so good at negotiating you can simultaneously be the good cop and the bad cop.

So let's have the Nobel Committee meet you in Singapore. Four prior administrations have failed, but you will not. Kim Jong-un's very existence depends on his nuclear weapons—as your very helpful National Security Advisor, John Bolton, pointed out by referencing Kaddafi and his demise after relinquishing nukes. But you, the Negotiator in Chief, will get Kim Jong-un to forget that, and hand over his nuclear weapons. Then the Nobel Committee can hand over your peace prize.

See you in Singapore!


Sincerely,
Will Friese
Phoenix

# SHAMELESSNESS

## 20

5/26/18

Dear President Trump:

I am sorry the Singapore Summit is not working out. It's surprising, considering how much planning your administration put into the process. But leave it to surly Kim Jung-un to spout off about war exercises off his coast and spoil your big moment. It's OK for you to talk about decimating North Korea—we are the USA, and that is expected. The whole exchange reminds me of a junior high school break-up. But I'm sure you and Kim Jung-un will be besties again soon.

It looks like the Nobel Peace Prize in on hold. No matter, I am in the process of recommending you for the Nobel Prize in Shamelessness. To support my recommendation, I will submit the following correspondence I recently received from you on the topic of Mother's Day.

After your usual opening formalities, you talked about how very special this day is, one on which we have "an opportunity to express our endless gratitude to the women who give their unyielding love and devotion to their families," honoring their "unending sacrifices to guide, protect, and nurture the success of their children."

You conclude with an inspiring reminder, asking us to every day "express our utmost respect, admiration, and appreciation" for our mothers and their "sacred gifts of life and unconditional love." I am especially a fan of the final sentence, even if it runs the risk of employing too many superlatives: "Whether we became their children through birth, adoption, or foster care, we know the unmatched power of the love, dedication, devotion, and wisdom of our mothers."

However, we must agree there's an irony underlying the thesis of your letter. You say Mother's Day is an opportunity to "express our utmost respect"? This begs the question: how does grabbing Mom by the pussy express our utmost respect? (Or do only non-mothers receive this treatment?) Your lack of introspection and your ability to say things that completely contradict your behavior are estimable qualities. They leave you unrestrained, primed to make America great again, and certainly a clear shoo-in for the Nobel Prize in Shamelessness.

*Congratulations!*
*Will Friese*
*Phoenix*

## 21

## GOLD STAR FAMILIES

5/29/18

Dear President Trump:

I write in reference to a communication I received from you on Memorial Day weekend. You reminded us that we owe a "debt of gratitude" to those who died fighting for our country and that we should "pause as a Nation to pay tribute to the brave men and women who have made the ultimate sacrifice to protect and defend our precious liberties." You also shared your plans to visit Arlington National Cemetery and "participate in a wreath laying ceremony to honor the fallen." You write, "As we commemorate the legacy of our patriots who have given their lives for this country, we pray that God comforts their spouses, families, and friends."

In conclusion, you state that you and Melania "send our thoughts and prayers to all the Gold Star families who have lost a loved one in the fight to preserve freedom." It's on this point that I need to call your attention to an inaccuracy. I don't blame you for this oversight, since I assume you did not write the letter. (I doubt you can write anything, considering the way you speak.) But this sentiment clearly does not reflect your opinions. Certainly, you don't send your "thoughts and prayers" to *all* Gold Star families.

During the presidential campaign, you belittled Khizr and Ghazala Khan, Muslims and Gold Star parents of U.S. Army Captain Humayun Khan. Captain Khan was killed in 2004 by a car bomb in Iraq. I presume you did not like it when his father, Khizr, speaking at the Democratic National Convention, criticized your attitudes towards Muslims. You responded by disparaging his family. You questioned why Captain Khan's mother, Ghazala, didn't speak. You suggested that she was muzzled by her husband or by her faith. You compared the Khans' sacrifices to your sacrifice of working hard and creating jobs. Do people know how hard it is to create jobs when you have bone spurs?

So make sure your writers get it straight for Memorial Day in 2019. I suggest, "Melania and I send our thoughts and prayers to all the *non-Muslim* Gold Star families who have lost a loved one." You need to keep the hate and ignorance turned up or you may start losing support.

Sincerely,
Will Friese
Phoenix

# SAM BEE

#22

6/5/18

Dear President Trump:

Can you believe what Samantha Bee said about Ivanka? I cannot. She was trying to make a valid criticism regarding your new policy of separating refugee children from their parents. But she used the word "cunt," and nobody heard anything else. Are you still reading? Or is someone still reading this to you?

I loved when General Kelly, your chief of staff, said separating children from their parents was a deterrent. I did not realize he had a sense of humor. The violence in the refugees' countries is so bad that these refugees are willing to travel 1000 miles on foot to keep their children safe. Separation is no deterrent; they will suffer anything for their child's safety. I know that the real reason to separate them is spite. You are rightly upset that you are making America great again and foreigners are taking advantage of it. They need to go back to their homelands, roll up their sleeves, and fight those well-armed, violent gangs. They need to make their own countries great again or die trying. We can't take in everyone.

You need to stop comedians like Samantha Bee from using dirty words and upsetting innocent people like

Ivanka and everyone at Fox News. I know what you can do. Ms. Bee is a mother of three. Take away her children. If you can do it with the refugees, why not with mean, foul-mouthed comedians? That will stop her, and deter her ilk!

Sincerely,
Will Friese
Phoenix

# BRIDENSTINE

# #23

6/6/18

Dear President Trump:

*Business Insider* just published a shocking article about Jim Bridenstine, director of NASA. It said he changed his opinion on climate change because he "read a lot." Can you believe this? Somebody in your administration is reading and, worse, learning. You need to nip this outlandish behavior in the bud before it spreads to others in the administration. Who will start believing in climate change next? What if Scott Pruitt, the head of the EPA, begins to "read a lot"? Although that is unlikely, as it will be hard to get a book into the ass of the oil and gas industry, which is where Scott Pruitt's head is.

But what if the other ignoramuses in your administration start reading and become enlightened like Bridenstine? You need to keep your administration in the dark so they can continue to push your anti-environment, anti-education, anti-conservation, anti-family planning, anti-immigration, anti-net neutrality, anti-free trade, anti-fiscal responsibility, and anti-everything Obama agenda.

I recommend you issue an executive order that all outside information is to come only from *Fox and*

*Friends*, with the occasional phone call from Sean Hannity. If that is good enough for you, it is good enough for your administration.

Godspeed my President,
Will Friese
Phoenix

# SCOTT PRUITT

*#24*

7/7/18

Dear President Trump:

I want to express my sincere support for your ongoing effort to "drain the swamp." With the resignation of Scott Pruitt—your appointee as administrator of the EPA and member of your cabinet—you have rid the swamp of its worst creature. It's fun to laugh at some of his shenanigans and shortcomings. Let's review, for old times' sake. As Attorney General of Oklahoma, he sued the EPA. He is a climate change denier. There are investigations into the repeated use of EPA staff for personal gain and to help his family. He had locked down his floor of the EPA to limit access and protect himself.[3] He installed a $43,000 soundproof booth in his office for phone calls.[4] He spent more than $100,000 on first class airfare.[5] He spent 3.5 million on round-the-clock security and had

---

3  Carol Davenport and Eric Lipton, "Scott Pruitt Is Carrying Out His E.P.A. Agenda in Secret, Critics Say," *The New York Times*, August 11, 2017, nytimes.com.

4  Lisa Friedman, "E.P.A. Chief's $43,000 Phone Booth Broke the Law, Congressional Auditors Say," *The New York Times*, April 16, 2008, nytimes.com.

5  Emily Holden, Anthony Adragna, and Alex Guillen, "Pruitt Spent Over $105,000 on First-Class Flights," *Politico*, March 20, 2018, politico.com.

his staff drive him around DC to find his favorite hand lotion at multiple Ritz-Carlton locations.[6]

It must have been hard for you to let him go. With fourteen ongoing ethics investigations, he makes even your questionable actions look good. More importantly, he pushed your dirty deregulation agenda. Big Oil & Gas will miss him dearly. I wonder what will happen to Mr. Pruitt now. Perhaps Oil & Gas will bring him home. More likely they will cast him aside like a used condom after their orgasm of deregulation.

Let's get back to congratulating you on draining the swamp. Seven of your cabinet members have left. That is way better than Obama and Bush, who only had only four leave during each of their first two years. You have two more cabinet members with ethics issues: Ryan Zinke and Wilbur Ross. And you have two more that appear incompetent or inept: Betsy DeVos and Ben Carson. There are only 15 cabinet members (besides Vice President Pence). So you are on track to get rid of them all. Don't replace them. Keep the swamp drained! Can you get rid of Pence too? What does he do but stand back and look at you adoringly? It would be nice if he rolled up his sleeves once in a while and helped you "Make America Great Again." Just fire him too. You don't need him or anybody. You are Swamp Creature in Chief!

Sincerely,
Will Friese
Phoenix

---

6   Juliet Eilperin, Josh Dawsey, and Brady Dennis, "Pruitt enlisted security detail in picking up dry cleaning, moisturizing lotion." *Washington Post*, June 8, 2018, washingtonpost.com.

# TARIFF MAN

**#25**

12/31/18

Dear President Trump:

You recently said that you are a "Tariff Man." I'm sorry, but this confuses me. I know for a fact that you have no idea how a tariff works. You repeatedly indicate that you believe foreign companies pay for tariffs. Tariffs are actually paid by the domestic companies receiving the products. This cost usually gets passed on to the U.S. consumer. Come on! My high school daughters know more about tariffs than you. So if you don't know what a tariff is, how could you be a "Tariff Man"?

Hold on! You sly fox! You know you don't understand tariffs—you just don't care! You're just bullshitting. That's why we voted you into office. So you could shake up DC and drain the swamp with your amazing lack of understanding about the real world. You have no idea what you are doing; you never have. You are "Tariff Man"!

Faster than the Mueller investigation ...

More powerful than a border wall ...

Able to leap Sarah Sanders in a single bound ...

Look! Into the Oval Office! It's a moron!

It's a buffoon!

It's Tariff Man!


*Happy New Year.*
*Will Friese*
*Phoenix*

## SHUTDOWN

# #26

1/19/19

Dear President Trump:

Congratulations are in order. Way to think outside the box once again. The Clemson Tigers football team, winner of the 2018 national championship, visited the White House recently during the partial government shutdown. The kitchen was furloughed, but that's no matter for a great mind like yours. You came up with the brilliant idea to serve them Wendy's and Burger King. As if that was not enough, you also had pizza. I'm sure the team was elated to travel all the way to the White House for hamburgers (and pizza). I doubt they can get that stuff in South Carolina. I hope, someday, that I do something noteworthy enough to be rewarded with fast food in the White House.

Speaking of genius moves, the partial shutdown—in part over the border wall funding—is a political masterpiece. First of all, I love the way you switched the blame for the shutdown. With video cameras rolling, you said you would be happy to take responsibility for the shutdown. When the shutdown came, you said it was the Democrats' fault. So shrewd and it makes perfect sense. Why would you accept responsibility when you never accept responsibility for anything that goes awry? Besides, the Democrats are always at fault, so they should own up to it.

I know you don't really want a wall. It was not even your idea. Your staff came up with that one night to help keep you focused during a rally (wishful thinking). Great minds like yours can't focus with all those great ideas floating around. What you really want is the government shutdown. You have been slowly destroying our government and its institutions from day one. You filled your cabinet with lobbyists who put special interests before the country. You nominated a Supreme Court Justice that, under scrutiny, readily disassembled into his basest qualities. Your administration has censored agencies like the EPA and CDC and hindered their ability to fulfill their missions. You disregarded findings by the CIA and FBI. You belittled federal judges. You pardoned a supporter that was convicted of violating the Constitution. You repeatedly assailed news organizations and their journalists. You have praised autocrats and had secret conversations with Putin. Your constant lying and unpredictable behavior have decimated foreign and domestic respect for the office of the presidency. Perhaps your most brilliant move was when you looked directly at an eclipse of the sun. This contradicts what schoolteachers have been telling their students for generations, undermining their authority and limiting their teaching efficacy.

Alas, my President, dealmaker extraordinaire that you are, you may have to take matters into your own (small) hands, declare a national emergency, and get that border wall funded. Then you can get the government reopened. I know you don't think so, but the government does do some good things. This way, you can save face. Although I'm not sure yours is a face worth saving. Have you ever considered extending your comb-over forward and down a bit?

If the national emergency thing works for the wall, you can do it for other things. Coal is still in trouble. Declare a national emergency and make everyone use it. Hillary is still free. Declare a national emergency and bring her to justice. You get the idea. Don't forget the biggest crisis of all, a Democratic majority in the House of Representatives, led by a woman no less! Forget the border! Declare a national emergency and build a wall around the House of Representatives.

Sincerely,
Will Friese
Phoenix

# PRESIDENTIAL LIBRARY

## #27

1/26/19

Dear President Trump:

I am writing to offer you my unwavering support. I know you need it because by all accounts, you had a terrible week. Nancy Pelosi treated you like a little bitch and denied you the House of Representatives for the State of the Union Address. The FBI arrested your good buddy Roger Stone. Another cabinet member's ineptness came to light when Wilbur Ross suggested furloughed federal workers that live paycheck to paycheck should take out loans. And he thinks bananas cost 10 dollars. Does he do his grocery shopping at the mini bars in expensive hotel rooms? Lastly, as everyone knows and agrees, you completely caved on the shutdown. Did you get paid during the shutdown? I guess you were an "essential" employee, essential to the shutdown anyway. We could not have had it without you!

Don't despair! Opening the government was the right thing to do. Federal workers need to do things, like eat. I heard government workers were visiting food pantries. That surprised me. Why didn't you buy them fast food like you did for the Clemson Tigers? I guess federal workers are not as deserving as football players.

Well, I'm *not* writing to point out all your deficiencies ... LORD, there is not enough pen and paper. I wanted to point out something that might make you feel better. As president, you get to build a library in your name—a "library" is a place where they store books for people to read and borrow. I know, it would be quite hypocritical to have a modern building constructed in your honor if it's full of things that you despise. That is why I'm writing. You can start working on legislation for a building that is more representative of you. The first thing that comes to mind is a hamburger museum. There could be a sweet food court like at the Smithsonian Museum of the American Indian, which has diverse foods from all over the Americas. Your museum could have Wendy's, Burger King, McDonald's, and maybe Carl's Jr.

If that does not interest you—which seems unlikely— perhaps a wax museum populated by you and your associates. I envision several rooms. One room would have all your associates that have been indicted by the Mueller investigation. I know it's a lot of wax, but we are just getting started. The main attraction would be a large room with you in the center yelling, "You're Fired!" You would be surrounded by everyone who you've fired, who's had their career destroyed by you, or who simply had their soul transformed trying to forward your agenda—along these lines, you really should set Sarah Sanders free, she is not looking good. Another room (and this is just to get traffic) would be of all the women that have accused you of sexual harassment. The center exhibit would be Stormy Daniels, a rolled-up magazine in her hand, administering some well-deserved "justice" upon you, if you know what I mean.

So, my President, you see, it's not all bad. Just keep doing what you do and enjoy your presidency when and where you can. It will all be over before you know it.


Sincerely,
Will Friese
Phoenix

# UNITY

## 28

2/3/19

Dear President Trump:

I just heard that your theme for the State of the Union Address is going to be "Unity." I about fell out of my chair laughing. I hope the State of the Union Address is full of jokes like that. Let me help a little. Instead of opening with the standard "The state of the union is strong," try "The state of the union is open." It's a little shutdown joke to endear you to all those that are still mad at you. More importantly, because you are opening with a truthful statement, you will trick everyone into believing the whole speech will be truthful. Then you can lie and deceive your way through the rest of the evening and make me proud. I can't wait to hear how you have made America great again, even if it's not true!

Sincerely,
Will Friese
Phoenix

## EMOLUMENTS CLAUSE

#29

10/23/19

Dear President Trump:

I am sorry it has been a while since I've written one of my supportive letters. It seems like things are going quite well and you don't need me. You tricked the Democrats into wasting time on the impeachment inquiry so they can't focus on their socialist agenda. By pulling out of northern Syria, you helped another NATO member, Turkey, embrace Russia—that will get you a few points with your buddy Putin. Your lawyer extraordinaire, Rudy Giuliani, has two associates that were indicted, and their lawyers may use executive privilege in the defense. No lower court judges are buying your argument that you shouldn't have to release your taxes. It looks like that issue is finally going to a court with a couple of justices that owe you one, the Supreme Court. And lastly, Mick Mulvaney eloquently confirmed the Ukrainian quid pro quo issue and then told the press corps to "Get over it." It's all great news for you.

Something came up this week during the Doral/G7 fiasco that made me want to write. You said the emoluments clause of the Constitution was phony. This may be the most brilliant thing I have heard you say, and you have said many brilliant things. Similar to how you have identified parts of the media that are fake (everyone but Fox), you have now identified parts of the Constitution that are phony. You are the rebel America needs! You have failed to conform to the norms of the executive branch in almost every aspect of your administration. It was just a matter of time until you got around to the Constitution.

I for one am ready for the brave new world where President Trump alone decides right and wrong, good and bad, true and phony. Where would we be without you? We would be stuck with that phony Constitution, the basis of our democracy.

All hail Trump!

Sincerely,
Will Friese
Phoenix

PS: Thanks for letting Mick Mulvaney out. That was a lot of fun. I suspect we won't be hearing from him again for a while.

# BOO!

## 30

11/5/19

Dear President Trump:

Boo! Happy Halloween. I'm sure you are aware that Representative Katie Hill just resigned over allegations of a sexual relationship with a staff member. She gave a really good resignation speech, for a Democrat. Additionally, the CEO of McDonald's—I know this is old news because you are an avid consumer of McDonald's products—was just fired for having a consensual relationship with a subordinate. This just shows how dumb people are compared to you. They should have followed the lead of their president and had sex with a porn star or Playboy model. Then they could keep their jobs and maintain public support. At least this is what I thought until Halloween.

There were two events around Halloween that made me wonder about your public support: game 5 of the World Series and a UFC bout at Madison Square Garden. At those events you were surprisingly and summarily booed. Maybe at the World Series, they were mad you did not throw out the first pitch. Probably your bone spurs were acting up, and they kept you off the mound as they kept you out of Vietnam. I'm just as sure the pitch would have been a blazing strike as I am that you would have returned from Vietnam heavily decorated. I can understand a bunch of drunken baseball fans booing you, but not the UFC audience. That's your crowd. It made me realize that it must all be in the spirit of Halloween. They were not booing you, just saying "Boo!" to their esteemed president.

With Halloween over, we don't have to worry about those misunderstandings regarding friendly "Boo!"-ing. But to be safe, for a while you may want to keep your public appearances limited to your typical rallies. Your trusted, red-hatted compatriots won't boo or criticize or think critically. They will do the one thing they know how to do: fall in line and follow you over the cliff, into the abyss. Boo!

Sincerely,
Will Friese
Phoenix

# "O CAPTAIN! MY CAPTAIN!"

## 31

12/19/19

Dear President Trump:

I know you are upset about your impeachment. I would be too! Those stupid, lazy Democrats only brought two articles of impeachment. It's so unfair how they treat you. Andrew Johnson got eleven articles. Even Bill Clinton got four articles—that's because hard-working Republicans impeached him. All of your efforts over these last three years are almost completely unrecognized. There are a lot of other things you should have been impeached for. Here is a list, courtesy of editor David Leonhardt at *The New York Times* (your favorite newspaper): lying constantly, obstructing justice, encouraging criminal behavior, corruptly profiting off the office, and refusing to defend the United States against foreign attacks.[7]

There is one silver lining: it's clear the whole of the Republican Party is under your control now. Even Senate Majority Leader Mitch McConnell is dancing at the ends of your puppet strings. I watched the impeachment debate as Republican after Republican declared their objection. Is there even one free thinker in the bunch? They all need to sit down and watch *Dead Poets Society* (best

---

7  David Leonhardt, "Impeached," *The New York Times,* December 19, 2019, nytimes.com.

movie ever). The impeachment was so bizarre. I hoped that someone, recognizing the complete absurdity of the circumstance, would stand on their desk and shout "O Captain! My Captain!" No one did. And, sadly, it looks like this ship is going down.

Sincerely,
Will Friese
Phoenix

# NOBEL PRIZES

## 32

2/9/20

Dear President Trump:

You have rightly been acquitted of wrong-doing during your "perfect" phone call to President Volodymyr Zelensky of Ukraine when you "perfectly" asked him to intervene in our election. Now it's time to get back to business.

Stop wasting your time upsetting the good people at the National Prayer Breakfast with expletive-laden rants against the Democrats and get down to the business of keeping our country white, I mean safe. Yes, I am talking about immigration. Things are getting worse. The *Wall Street Journal* reported that immigrants have been awarded nearly 40% of the Nobel Prizes won by Americans in Chemistry, Medicine, and Physics since 2000.

Not only are immigrants taking our jobs, they are also taking our Nobel Prizes. If you can keep them out with your wall (assuming the winds stay low—I heard part fell over during a gentle breeze), then maybe there will be some Nobel Prizes left over for you. At least a Nobel Peace Prize, for keeping all the "bad hombres" from getting in here and disturbing our peace with their hard-working, faith-observing, family-rearing, tax-paying ways.

I have already written the Nobel Committee a recommendation for you.

Sincerely,
Will Friese
Phoenix

# LT. COL. ALEXANDER VINDMAN

#33

2/10/20

Dear President Trump:

It's becoming apparent that you have at least one flaw. I know it's hard to believe, but stay with me. It's geography. While speaking in Colorado last year, you asked the residents what they thought about the wall on their border. That was good for a laugh in Colorado. I bet it made the residents of New Mexico, on Colorado's southern border, nervous. They were just one presidential Sharpie stroke (à la Hurricane Dorian and Alabama) from a recreated map of the United States that no longer included New Mexico — you gotta save face somehow. When it was pointed out to you that Colorado is not a border state, you pretended you were just kidding, and New Mexicans breathed a sigh of relief.

I was gonna let that slide; however, after the Super Bowl, you congratulated the State of Kansas on the victory of the Kansas City Chiefs. No doubt there are plenty of Chief fans in Kansas City, Kansas, but my God, Mr. President, the Chiefs are from Kansas City, Missouri. I'm sure there are plenty of residents that would love to "show you" that on a map.

Something must be done. I don't mind you being wrong about tariffs, tax cuts, climate change, healthcare, skin color, etc. ... but you gotta get the location of the Super Bowl Champion right! So I'm sending you a puzzle map of the United States. My kids used to love it. Alas, they are grown and no longer need it. Since it appears you still have a few areas in which to grow, it would be best if you had it now.

The puzzle should be enclosed with this letter. If not, blame your staff and fire someone. And make sure you fire one of that staff member's siblings also. Just like impeachment witness Lt. Col. Alexander Vindman, who you recently fired. He didn't even steal a puzzle, just did his job and obeyed Congress. And you fired his twin brother, Lt. Col. Yevgeny Vindman, a lawyer, who did even less than that. Seems a little bit capricious, but it sure sends a message. Maybe the people of New Mexico should be nervous.

Sincerely,
Will Friese
Phoenix

## 34

# ROGER STONE

2/12/20

Dear President Trump:

I want to congratulate you on your efforts to support Roger Stone. He is your old friend and informal advisor who, like a lot of your associates, is heading to jail. When he was indicted, you tweeted it was "a travesty of justice." I know what you meant. Not that justice was ill-served, but that the Justice Department is a travesty. Roger Stone was working for you, and, HELLO, so is the Department of Justice! I can only imagine your frustration when the apolitical career prosecutors on the case recommended seven to nine years of jail for Mr. Stone (out of a maximum of 50 years.)

This is where you got to work. You had the Attorney General, Bill Barr, who fortunately has a smaller moral compass than you—he must have been hard to find—walk back the prosecutors' recommendation. This angered the prosecutors. Apparently, they still believe in the ethos established after Watergate, whereby the Justice Department should only serve the law and not be used as a political tool. The prosecutors Aaron S. J. Zelinsky, Adam Jed, and Michael Marando withdrew from the case; Jonathon Kravis resigned. But you need not worry about that. Career government employees don't matter. Ethics don't matter. Justice does not matter. All that matters is you and your supporters.

Sincerely, your biggest supporter in Phoenix,
Will Friese

# CORONAVIRUS

**#35**

2/27/20

Dear President Trump:

We all know you are a huge germaphobe—I once saw you do the Samba trying to evade a mosquito. So it is a testament to your cost-cutting nature that your administration eliminated the pandemic response team in 2018 and cut the CDC budget for global disease outbreak prevention by 80%, including funding in China. Gotta get the money for The Wall from somewhere.

So thank goodness you put Mike Pence in charge of coordinating our response to the coronavirus. The virus may turn out to be even more dangerous than the Mexicans. Pence has a bit of a weakness, though, in fighting natural problems. He does not seem to be a man of science. There is reason to believe he supports conversion therapy for gay people, and he initially refused to distribute free needles in Indiana during the AIDS epidemic. But he has one strength: a steely-eyed gaze. Remember when you sent him to South Korea, adorned in a bomber jacket, to stare across the demilitarized zone at North Korea? We let the North Koreans know we don't take their nuclear threats lightly. That worked well. We have not been nuked. So set Vice President Pence up at the Statue of Liberty, to look out across New York Harbor and stare down all the viruses coming ashore. That will be at least as successful as conversion therapy.

Tell the vice president not to forget the bomber jacket. It may be a bit brisk still on Liberty Island this time of year.


Sincerely,
Will Friese
Phoenix

## CUT RATE BIG

## 36

3/4/20

Dear President Trump:

Coronavirus is here and it's hurting the thing you love most: the stock market. Your response was to ask the Federal Reserve to lower interest rates. You are a true leader. It's not because you asked to lower rates. That was naked political pandering meant to get the economy in its best shape for your reelection. You are a leader because of the way you asked—a way that all of your supporters could understand. You are a modern Shakespeare. You tweeted that the Federal Reserve needed to "cut rate big."

It is this elegant speech that got you elected. I thought of a few other phrases that you could use to get your message out and secure your reelection.

Build Wall Tall

Buy Gun Easy

Abort Baby Never

Purge Staff Small

Slash Tax Tiny

Tariff China All

Worry Climate Silly

Watch Fox Long

Cheat Wife Lots

Grow Hand Bigly

Tan Skin Orange

Sincerely,
Will Friese
Phoenix

# SOCIAL DISTANCING

## #37

4/5/20

Dear President Trump:

A poll was reported on April 1st by *Newsweek*—probably a joke, definitely fake news—that said Americans don't trust you about when to end social distancing. They are probably thinking about your righteous desire for packed pews at Easter. By the way, Jews were feeling a little left out when you said that. Is it OK to welcome in Elijah to Passover Seder if the Christians are packing the church? He can even wear a cloth mask. Argh, I digress! Besides, it's a moot point; the guy never shows, which is fine, more wine for the rest of us.

Once again, you are misunderstood and not given credit where it is due. Over a month ago, when the rest of your staff was working on a coherent American response to the pandemic—I assume they are still working on it, given the general lack of coherence—you were on the golf course fundraising.

I am sure to some that seemed selfish and shortsighted, but actually you were leading by example. Sure, you were golfing and fundraising, you were also setting a national example for social distancing. There are always at least 100 yards between you and the next group. Sometimes more. I assume you are a big hitter and use the championship tees. That is at least 300 yards of social distance. Most of us could not even dream of big, beautiful, perfect social distancing like that. You are such a strong leader.

No need to worry about shelter in place. Here in Arizona, golfing is an essential business. At least one governor is paying attention to your example.

See you on the links. Fore!!!!


Sincerely,
Will Friese
Phoenix

# HYDROXYCHLOROQUINE

## 38

4/7/20

Dear President Trump:

"What do you have to lose?" you recently said about using an unproven drug, hydroxychloroquine, in terminally ill COVID-19 patients. And then you added, "But what do I know? I'm not a doctor." Well, I *am* a doctor, and I will tell you what I know. You are a genius. A genius that can see through the complexities of a matter and dumb it down for the rest of us. You don't need information to tell you what's right; you use your gut to make a decision. When a reporter asked the opinion of the doctor standing next to you, Anthony Fauci, MD, you prevented his response. That was smart. He would have droned on about side effects, drug interactions, the need for peer-reviewed studies, and the risk of creating shortages for patients for whom the drug is clearly beneficial.

"What do you have to lose?" It is so persuasive the way you say it. I bet you used that a lot in past business dealings. Is that how you got people to invest in the Taj Mahal casino and your other bankrupted businesses?

Did they lose anything?

Sincerely,
William Friese, M.D.
Phoenix

## DUMB DON

# #39

4/25/20

Dear President Trump:

Well, I guess you had it coming. With all the nicknames you have given others—Crooked Hillary, Sleepy Joe, Lyin' Ted—eventually an equally appropriate nickname would befall you. A friend of mine, now a former friend of mine, nicknamed you "Dumb Don." I have to admit, it has a nice ring to it. I will not tell anyone about the new nickname. Hopefully it will not catch on.

You could help your cause a bit and stop saying batshit crazy stuff, like how the administration is looking into injecting disinfectant into COVID patients and bringing UV light inside the body to kill the virus. It is hard for me and others to defend your genius when you say stuff that is blatant nonsense. There's lots of ammunition for your new nickname. See the list below, tabulated by Richard Hine[8]:

February 10: "A lot of people think that goes away in April with the heat—as the heat comes in."

February 24: "The Coronavirus is very much under control in the USA ... Stock Market starting to look very good to me!"

---

8   Used with permission from Richard Hine, "American Idiot, a running list of the dumbest things Trump has said about the coronavirus," https://thedailyedge.substack.com/p/american-idiot.

<u>February 25</u>: "I think that's a problem that's going to go away... They have studied it. They know very much. In fact, we're very close to a vaccine."

<u>March 6</u>: "Anybody right now, and yesterday, anybody that needs a test gets a test. They're there. And the tests are beautiful ... the tests are all perfect like the letter was perfect. The transcription was perfect. Right? This was not as perfect as that but pretty good."

<u>March 6</u>: "I like this stuff. I really get it. People are surprised that I understand it ... Every one of these doctors said, 'How do you know so much about this? Maybe I have a natural ability. Maybe I should have done that instead of running for president."

<u>March 6</u>: "When I was hearing the amount of people that died with the flu, I was shocked to hear it ... I would have said, 'Does anybody die of the flu?' I didn't know people died from the flu."

<u>March 12</u>: "We need a little separation until such time as this goes away. It's gonna go away, it's gonna go away ... But in the meantime, we want to lose as few people as possible, so important."

<u>March 12</u>: "Frankly, the testing has been going very smooth ... we've done a good job on testing."

<u>March 15</u>: "This is a very contagious virus. It's incredible. But it's something that we have tremendous control over."

<u>March 27</u>: "You can call it a germ. You can call it a flu. You can call it a virus ... I'm not sure anybody even knows what it is."

<u>April 10:</u> "The germ has gotten so brilliant that the antibiotic can't keep up with it."

<u>April 18:</u> "If I wasn't elected, the world would be over."

This is only part of the list, but you get the idea. At least the last one is true. I am begging you to start up that pre-coronavirus stable genius again and start talking sense, or you might get yourself a new nickname.

Sincerely,
Will Friese
Phoenix

# #40

## SARCASM

5/2/20

Dear President Trump:

Remember about a week ago, when you were spit-balling COVID-19 cures with Dr. Deborah Birx at a press conference? Something about injecting disinfectant and swallowing UV light. As a doctor, I would like to say—and I think I speak for all doctors—that there was a huge sigh of relief in the medical community. The stable genius in the White House, with the big beautiful brain, who really gets this stuff, was going to help. Our comparatively small brains would not have to work so hard and feverishly towards treatments and a vaccine.

We know you have our country to run and other countries to antagonize—China comes to mind (purveyor of COVID-19, aka the China Virus, leaked straight from its secret labs). We are so grateful that you can dedicate some time between watching Fox News and watching more Fox News to help our cause. Just as we were making plans to quit our research because you were on the case, you pulled the rug out from under us and said the following day that you were being "sarcastic." Then you discontinued your press conferences.

Granted, your first ideas were a bit, um ... well, let's just say, not compatible with biology as it is currently understood. Clearly Dr. Birx did not understand your genius. She looked like she was trying to hold down a big vomit during the press conference. But that is how breakthroughs are made. You gotta think outside the box, something you are really good at. I mean, you can't even see the box from where you are positioned.

Lastly, I have to call you out on your use of the word "sarcastic" to explain your cutting-edge COVID therapy recommendations. Sarcasm is something I consider myself an expert on, and I don't think you really understand it. First of all, when being sarcastic, you are making a point at someone else's expense. You are mocking them. What point were you trying to make at the conference and who were you mocking? My second piece of evidence that you do not understand sarcasm is your uniformly positive responses to my letters. Here is your last response to my letter about your new nickname, "Dumb Don":

*"President Donald J. Trump believes the strength of our country lies in the spirit of the American people and their willingness to stay informed and get involved.*

*President Trump appreciates your taking the time to reach out. Sincerely,*

*The Office of Presidential Correspondence"*

I think it's pretty obvious by this response that you don't understand the true nature of my letter(s). Wait a second ... you do understand, and your response is totally sarcastic. You don't care about the populace being informed. You thrive on a misinformed, uninvolved public. You don't appreciate my time; you could not give a shit. You are mocking me. I understand. You are the master; I am the apprentice.

I want you to know that I truly appreciate your taking the time to respond to my letters.


Sincerely,
Will Friese
Phoenix

# PRESS SECRETARY

#41

5/4/20

Dear President Trump:

I am writing to let you know about something that is bothering me. No, it's not the COVID-19 lockdown. However, a "Liberate Arizona" tweet from the Liberator in Chief would be appreciated. I am writing about your new press secretary, Kayleigh McEnany, who held her first press conference last Friday.

First of all, what is the point of a press conference or a press secretary? Your last press secretary, Stephanie Grisham, never had a press conference during her nine-month tenure. The public is perfectly fine with getting the information unfiltered via presidential tweets and hours-long presidential briefings.

Secondly, and disturbingly, Ms. McEnany told reporters, "I will never lie to you. You have my word on that." How can the Trump administration communicate with the public without lying? Think about that for a minute. Sorry, I forgot about your short attention span. Think about that for a few seconds. Still with me? Your presidency was founded on misinformation and lies. She can't tell the truth. You can't tell the truth. We don't want the truth and, we would not know what to do with the truth if you gave it to us.

For the sake of your presidency and our country, I hope that she was lying when she said she would never lie.

Honestly,
Will Friese
Phoenix

# OVERLY PRESCRIPTIVE

#42

5/9/20

Dear President Trump:

More thanks to your administration for the creation of the great new catch phrase, "overly prescriptive," which was recently used to accurately describe the CDC guidelines for reopening the country. It stands in contrast to your administration's more manageable guidelines, which could be described as "not-at-all prescriptive" —I made that one up. It got me thinking about all the things in my life that are OP (overly prescriptive). Traffic laws, for example. Totally OP, especially when I am late for work. Speed limits, stoplights, "Do Not Enter" signs— they just slow me down.

The CDC's recommendations for churches were particularly OP. "Governments have a duty to instruct the public on how to stay safe during this crisis and can absolutely do so without dictating to people how they should worship God," said Roger Severino, the director of the Department of Health and Human Services Office for Civil Rights, who once oversaw the DeVos Center for Religion and Civil Society at the Heritage Foundation.[9] Has the CDC not heard of separation of church and

9  Abby Goodnough and Maggie Haberman, "White House Rejects C.D.C.'s Coronavirus Reopening Plan." *The New York Times.* May 7, 2020, nytimes.com.

state? Churchgoers know how to take care of themselves. Last April, a woman exiting church services was asked if she was concerned about contracting and spreading COVID-19. "No," she replied, "I'm covered in Jesus' blood."[10] As a doctor, I should note that the evidence supporting the immunological properties of the Blood of Jesus is completely anecdotal, and there have been no controlled randomized trials. Although, it is probably more effective and definitely safer than hydroxychloroquine. Those hoping for quick adoption of the "Blood of Jesus" vaccine should know that there will be severe supply chain issues.

Well, I'm off to work, running red lights, hopping medians, and driving the opposite way down the street. Traffic laws are OP when I have bigger considerations. I'm definitely getting to work on time ... assuming I get there at all.

Sincerely,
Will Friese
Phoenix

---

10 David Matthews, "'I'm covered in Jesus' blood': Ohio Churchgoers Claim Coronavirus Immunity," *New York Daily News*, April 5, 2020, nydailynews.com.

# PELOSI PRESIDENCY

#43

5/14/20

Dear President Trump:

I guess it was bound to happen, considering you don't wear a mask or socially distance: COVID-19 has come to the White House. Katie Miller, Mike Pence's press secretary and wife of the architect of your evil immigration policy, Stephen Miller, has tested positive. What if Stephen Miller gets sick? Who is going to fill his xenophobic shoes? I hope he can get on Zoom and send in the hate electronically. If not, this place is going to fill up with COVID coughing immigrants.

Per the Presidential Succession Act of 1947, if you and the vice president become infected and incapacitated (more so than usual), then Speaker of the House Nancy Pelosi becomes the acting president. Thursday, your new press secretary was asked what the plan is to assist Speaker Pelosi, if she should become acting president. "That's not even something that we're addressing," she stated. Why would you address that, considering you are barely addressing COVID-19? Besides, a "Pelosi Presidency"? How do you plan for the end of the world?

Stay healthy!
Will Friese
Phoenix

# ANOTHER ONE BITES THE DUST

## 44

5/18/20

Dear President Trump:

Lately, I have been happily humming the Queen classic "Another One Bites the Dust." You reminded me of it when you fired another inspector general, Steve Linick, late Friday. He led the Office of the Inspector General at the State Department. He is the fourth inspector general you have dismissed since April 3rd this year.

The IG (inspector general) is a position in many governmental and military departments or agencies that ensures proper compliance, conducts audits, uncovers fraud and waste, etc. It seems to me that this is an outdated position. Your impeachment trial proved that you and your administration can do anything you want. Hell, if the Senate does not care about you inviting a foreign power to interfere in our presidential election, then why should anyone care about *anything* you do? What is the point of oversight?

Inspector General Linick had it coming. He opened an investigation into your subservient secretary of state, Mike Pompeo. Secretary Pompeo toed the line during your impeachment: he failed to support his staff when they came under fire for testifying against you. So it is only right that you support him now that he is under fire from the IG. Sing it with me: Hey—hey—hey—another IG bites the dust!

I can't wait until the Supreme Court rules on the case you brought claiming you are immune from criminal investigation while in office. Once they rule in your favor, you can take your seat on the throne and finally be King Trump. Then you will not have to fire any other IGs; you can just reassign them as court jesters.

Sincerely,
Will Friese
Phoenix

## WINTER RULES

#45

5/27/20

Dear President Trump:

More congratulations are in order as you continue to forge new paths in the discipline of false and misleading claims. As of last month, you had made over 18,000 false and misleading claims[11] —that is 15 per day. Simply amazing! No president will ever outdo that. I bet you are giving Vladimir Putin and Kim Jong-un a run for their money. Those two autocrats have it easy. They don't have to deal with the "fake" news like you do here. In their countries, they have *real* fake news.

This amazing feat has been accomplished even while spending one in five days on the golf course. Do you cheat on the golf course? That's a rhetorical question. I bet you multitask and think about lies while you putt. It probably relaxes you and allows you to play better. I find golfing brings out my dishonest side too. Just like Judge Smails in *Caddyshack*, I am often "interfered with" and don't count all my shots. I always play by "winter rules" even in the summer.[12] Well, enough about my dishonesty, let's get back to yours.

---

11 Glenn Kessler, Salvador Rizzo, and Meg Kelly, "President Trump Made 18,000 False or Misleading Claims in 1,170 Days," *Washington Post*, April 14, 2020, washingtonpost.com.

12 Ted Knight as Judge Smails, *Caddyshack* (1980), directed by Harold Ramis, www.youtube.com/watch?v=MCvgMNnM3OA.

You may need to tone things down a bit. You claimed that one of your fiercest critics, MSNBC host Joe Scarborough, killed someone. Did you get that idea from Q, the anonymous far-right conspiracy theorist? Then you said that mail-in voting would be rife with fraud. Even Twitter has started adding fact-checking labels to your tweets. This rightly inflamed you, and you threatened to shut down Twitter. We can't have Twitter and other social media platforms sullied with facts. But don't come down too hard on Twitter. Give them a good scare, but remember, these are the platforms that enable you to spread your false and misleading claims. We have to keep your record going. Q says to his followers, "do your own research." You know where his followers do their "research"? Twitter, Facebook, et al. You have your base convinced that mainstream news is fake. Keep Twitter open so you can just feed them whatever "research" you want.

Oh, one more thing, on the latest piece of misinformation you put out. Are you infected with the coronavirus? You said, "And I tested very positively in another sense—this morning, yeah. I tested positively toward negative, right? So, I tested perfectly this morning ... Meaning I tested negative ... But that's a way of saying it: positively toward the negative."

So you tested negative? I hope so, but I'm not sure I trust you. I think I will do my own research.

Sincerely,
Will Friese
Phoenix

## 46

# LOOTING AND SHOOTING

6/1/20

Dear President Trump:

I am excited to know that, for sure, you are reading my letters. In my last letter, I asked you to tone down your tweets a bit. And tone down you did. On May 29th, you tweeted, "when the looting starts, the shooting starts." Which is so much better than what you probably wanted to say: when the looting starts, the lynching starts.

Twitter blocked the tweet because it "glorified violence." I was disappointed because you denied knowing the racist origins of that saying, and thereby, you denied the racism inherent in your tweet. Why? Have you not made racism okay? A big part of your goal to "Make America Great Again" was to "Make America Racist Again." In reality, you have simply enabled a racist country to be more overtly racist, but that's not catchy and it won't fit on a red hat.

There is no denying your progress in promoting racism. Look at that crazy white woman in Central Park who was so comfortable with her racism that she continued her racist rant while being filmed and even called in the police. She felt threatened by a Black, binocular-wearing birdwatcher who asked her to comply with posted regulations to leash her dog. This is one of the most racist things I have ever witnessed. She felt threatened by a birdwatcher. I don't care if a guy is twelve feet tall and screaming at me to give him all my money. If he is wearing binoculars around his neck, he's not getting anything from me but a hearty laugh.

So as COVID-19 continues to ravage our country and we pass the mark of 100,000 infections, and as the economy continues to whither and unemployment soars past 15% toward 20%, take solace in a job well done on the topic of racism.

Sincerely,
Will Friese
Phoenix

# PRESIDENT OF LAW AND ORDER

#47

6/4/20

Dear President Trump:

The self-proclaimed "President of Law and Order" has arrived in Lafayette Square! LAFAYETTE! You and your men are so strong! Those unarmed peaceful protesters fled like cowards before the heavily armed, militarized police. All that body armor they were wearing makes sense: they were running so fast through the protesters, they might have tripped and fallen to the hard pavement. It's good that you are setting an example, right in your backyard, for the state governors, whom you recently derided on a video conference call: "If you don't dominate, you're wasting your time. They're going to run all over you, you'll look like a bunch of jerks." More concisely, "most of you are weak."[13]

I watched a video where a cameraman got a shield thrust in his gut as he stood there filming. He got off easy. His companion was lucky too. She only got a club to the back—as she ran away.

Why are they protesting again?

Thanks to William Barr for ordering that operation. It went so well that even Chuck Schumer was impressed.

---

13 "READ: President Trump's call with US governors over protests." *CNN.* 6/1/2020, cnn.com.

He nicknamed him, "General Barr." It's funny because he left out "attorney." Attorney General Barr has been quite effective at sordid tasks like clearing nonviolent, unarmed protesters, rewriting investigations such as the Mueller report, and un-confessing federal criminals like Michael Flynn.

Gassing and clearing those protesters was absolutely necessary for you to get a picture in front of Saint John's Church. You had to stop those nasty rumors that you were scared and hiding in the White House bunker. You had to show your strength. The picture is glorious and was well worth trampling the rights of the protesters. It shows you alone holding up the Bible. I contrast it to other images of large groups protesting. Standing alone, it is clear how much stronger you are. You don't need anyone else. Weaker people need to mass together. You have the Bible on your side. Just like Kim Jung-un of North Korea and the Kings of England with their divine authority, you also act on the Bible's authority. The protesting masses merely have clenched fists in the air—are they mad that someone took their Bibles? What is their authority?

You said that you are the "'President of Law and Order," but don't sell yourself short. I say you are the "King of Justice," as once again you show how you can rise above the people.

Sincerely,
Will Friese
Phoenix

PS: Next time get Ivanka or Press Secretary Kayleigh McEnany to clean up the photo-op site a little. There is an empty cup on the step right next to you. The protesters probably left it there as they were forcibly removed. Lawbreakers!

# THE APPRENTICE

#48

6/17/20

Dear Master Trump:

Your apprentice, Mike Pence, is progressing nicely in the art of lying. On June 16th, the *Wall Street Journal* published an op-ed, authored by Pence, entitled "There Isn't a Coronavirus 'Second Wave.'" A masterful, misleading statement that is technically true. We are actually having a continued, unmitigated first wave.[14] On June 15th, *The New York Times* reported that Vice President Pence encouraged the governors to explain to their residents that the increased rise in cases is due to increased testing.[15] Another artful lie that demonstrates your influence.

I am a little surprised that you're having so much success with Pence lying because your real specialty is bullshitting. To be clear, lying is deliberately deceiving for a purpose. Bullshitting is just saying stuff with no regard as to its veracity.[16] For example, you recently said, "If we

14 Jane Bradley, et al. "U.S. ROUNDUP. Pence dismisses fears of a second wave. Fauci says the U.S. is still in its first." *The New York Times*, 6/17/20.

15 Katie Rodgers and Jonathon Martin. "Pence Misleadingly Blames Coronavirus Spikes on Increased Testing." *The New York Times*, 6/15/20.

16 Harry G Frankfurt. *On Bullshit*. Princeton University Press, 2005.

stop testing right now, we'd have very few cases, if any." [17] That is a big piece of bullshit. It is almost nonsensical; it is akin to believing that if you look away from the sun, it disappears. Some might think you have not mastered the concept of object permanence—most do by eight months of age. I know that you are just bullshitting.

But be careful, my President, of your pretty little liar in training. He wants your job. What if you disappear and Pence comes up with a great lie, based on his master's training? Something like, "If we stop looking for Trump right now, we won't miss him, at all."

In the meantime, the two of you are going to have to put your full heads of hair together and come up with some better lies (or bullshit). Data from one of the hospitals I work at shows COVID hospitalizations have doubled in about three weeks. The lie, that increased testing leads to increased cases, can't be applied to increased admissions. So give us another whopper that allows us to ignore reality and go out into the world unafraid, unmasked, and unwitting.

Sincerely,
Will Friese
Phoenix

---

17 Katie Rodgers and Jonathon Martin. "Pence Misleadingly Blames Coronavirus Spikes on Increased Testing." *The New York Times*, 6/15/20.

# SPITEFUL NATION

## 49

6/20/20

Dear President Trump:

Ours is a spiteful nation. I am not sure how you get up every morning, put on that long red tie, comb over your hair, tan for a bit, watch *Fox and Friends*, take in a few more hours of "executive time," and then face the nation with all the determination needed to set us straight. On further consideration, I am not sure why you get up at all. But if you get up, I'm here to support you. First, let's review the spite.

The Supreme Court let you down twice in two days. First, it extended the Civil Rights Act to prevent discrimination in the workplace against gay and trans-gender employees. Second, it ruled that the Dreamers, people brought to the U.S. illegally as children, could continue living, working, and paying taxes under the DACA program. The court refused your decision to end the program because your reasoning was "arbi-trary and capricious." Thank you Chief "Master of the Obvious," Roberts! Arbitrary and Capricious are your watchwords. If you had a coat of arms, "Arbitrary" and "Capricious" would be right there in bold letters next to a fearsome dragon. You tweeted, "Do you get the impression that the Supreme Court doesn't like me?" And the people tweeted back, "Yes, there are a lot of us that don't like you." That is the price you pay for being ahead of your time ... or are you behind? Well, you are clearly somewhere else.

You later told the *Wall Street Journal* that you thought some Americans are wearing masks to express their disapproval of you.[18] That was a mistake. As soon as you said that, Governor Gavin Newsome jumped on the bandwagon and is having all of California wear masks and thumb their (hopefully) covered noses at you. Our governor, Doug Ducey, was slightly less spiteful when he decided to stop preventing local municipalities from having mask requirements. As we speak, major cities are moving against you (and requiring masks). It is a clear demonstration of your political strength that our governor, despite an exponential increase in cases and an 85% ICU occupancy, refuses to protect his residents. Because, you know, he does not want to disappoint you. Priorities!

Hydroxychloroquine, your favorite ingestible drug after Clorox, had its COVID emergency authorization revoked secondary to ineffectiveness ... even after they saw that it did not kill you. At least they didn't take your Clorox away. Twitter blocked your retweets of Jayda Fransen, leader of the far-right group Britain First—possible Nazism issue. Facebook took down a video you posted—copyright and manipulation issue. Lastly, Judge Royce C. Lamberth refused to block the distribution of John Bolton's book. Bit of a silver lining there,

---

18 Michael C. Bender, "Trump Talks Juneteenth, John Bolton, Economy in WSJ Interview," *Wall Street Journal*, June 19, 2020, wsj.com.

though—it appears to be an excellent primer on how to use the presidency for personal and political gain.

You still have lots of supporters. AMC Theater's CEO Adam Aron said, ironically, "We did not want to be drawn into a political controversy. We thought it might be counterproductive if we forced mask wearing on those people who believe strongly that it is not necessary." Sadly, there was a bit of a backlash and he has reversed course. Soon you will be in Tulsa, basking in the glow of your beloved supporters, some of whom have been camping out for two days. That does not seem reasonable. You better check their temperatures before you let them in.

Oh, and stay off the ramps and use a straw for your glass of water. We don't want you to look silly like you did at West Point last week.

Sincerely,
Will Friese
Phoenix

# THE ALBATROSS

#50

6/23/20

Dear President Trump:

You were just here in Phoenix. I was a little surprised you did not reach out to me despite all my support; it's just as well. My support has waned.

I saw pictures of teens waiting outside for your rally, most congregating closely, without masks. I thought about going and setting up a small stand labeled "Reserve Your ICU Bed Here." I would inform them about the rapidly escalating utilization of our healthcare resources as our economy reopens. ICU bed usage has increased from 60% in March to almost 90% now.

Vice President Pence recently said the increase in cases was secondary to "hotspots." He should have said they were secondary to "hotstates." Arizona is reporting increases in almost every county. You can't fit the Grand Canyon State into a "spot." Yes, the Grand Canyon is in Arizona.

You said at the Tulsa rally, "I said to my people, 'Slow the testing down please.'" Your campaign said you were kidding. But how in any sense is that funny or even satirical? Seriously, I know a little bit about funny and a lot about satire.[19] If you think you have a sense of humor; well, that is funny, I will give you that.

As a physician, I have had enough of your ineptitude. Data continue to support that masks and testing are effective strategies. As you slow testing, you also refuse to wear a mask. You see the mask as an Albatross. You probably don't understand that metaphor. Look it up.

> Ah! well a-day! what evil looks
> Had I from old and young!
> Instead of the cross, the Albatross
> About my neck was hung.[20]

You view wearing a mask as admission of a problem that is not under control. A burden that you have failed. A weakness made evident. Your narcissism has turned the mask into a symbol instead of an effective means to combat the spread of a pandemic. So people are choosing not to wear it. Not on its merits but on its symbolism. Furthermore, your lack of mask-wearing lends credence to the belief that things are getting better. This in turn leads to inaction or even counterproductive action. Take our Governor Ducey, for example. He restricted our municipalities from requiring masks. As soon as the restriction was lifted, most municipalities ordered mask-wearing. His restrictions were a form of tyranny, not leadership. This is what you sow.

---

19 William Friese, *Dear President Trump: 50 Satirical Letters from Phoenix to the White House* (2020), letters #1– #49.

20 Samuel Taylor Coleridge, *The Rime of the Ancient Mariner*, 1798 (London: Robert Riviere & Son, 1909), lines 139–142.

The two hospitals I work at send out daily communications. The most distressing thing they highlight, besides the relentless rise in COVID cases, is the emotional stress and fatigue suffered by a completely dedicated staff. We have the knowledge; we don't have the leadership.

> Water, water, everywhere,
> And all the boards did shrink;
> Water, water, everywhere,
> Nor any drop to drink.[21]

The irony of trying to save the economy at the expense of not containing COVID is that an unrestrained COVID will cause far greater economic harm. Good luck with your reelection. You can no longer count on me for support; this is my last letter to you. Just as you have left us on our own, I take my leave of you.

*Sincerely,*
*Will Friese*
*Phoenix*

---

21 Coleridge, *The Rime*, lines 119–122.

# EPILOGUE 7/23/20

I have concluded my letter writing, but the absurdity continues front and center. A few things almost pulled me off the bench and wrecked the nice round number of 50 letters. The press secretary just said, "The science should not stand in the way of this," referring to children returning to school during the pandemic; federal agents beat up a protesting Navy veteran, Christopher David, in Portland; the administration bashed Dr. Fauci, White House coronavirus advisor, for being "alarmist" regarding the coronavirus; Trump commuted the sentence of his recently convicted friend, Roger Stone; and COVID data gathering was taken away from the CDC and given to the Department of Health and Human Services where it can be controlled by the administration. The nonsense will continue until Trump is voted out.

One last piece of nonsense. In March of 2017, Ryan Zinke, former Congressman from Montana and Trump appointee for the Secretary of the Interior, arrived at his post in Washington on horseback. The horse was named Tonto. Tonto looked pretty fresh, so I don't think Zinke rode him the whole way from Montana. Less than two years later, Zinke resigned amid multiple ethics investigations, one of which had been referred to the Justice Department. I wonder, when Zinke departed Washington, did he do that on horseback also? Did he ride Tonto off into the sunset?

Which begs another question: if there is some order to the universe, and Trump is voted out in November, how will he exit? I hope Tonto is still available.

THE SATIRE CONTINUES
@DEARTRUMPBOOK ON TWITTER AND FACEBOOK.

# ACKNOWLEDGMENTS

My ever-supportive family, Staci, Zoe, Emma, and Corin, reviewed many versions of these letters. Zoe was editor in chief and did the bulk of the reviews. Corin filled her older sisters' shoes admirably when they were both abroad for gap years. My "in-house," conscripted editorial staff made the material infinitely more readable and I am grateful for their help and the opportunity to spend time with them on this project. My left-leaning friends and extended family leant an ear and provided positive feedback to keep me inspired. Mike Mathewson motivated me to publish. My siblings, Rebecca Rodskog and Whit Friese, provided support and guidance during the publishing process. The cover design was by Corin and Corey Ciszek. Their work added legitimacy to the project I did not think possible. Sandy Sullivan provided excellent copyediting. She caught many mistakes and greatly improved the final product with her tweaks to the text. Amie McCracken designed a beautiful interior and was very gracious with this first time, often ignorant, author. For the fair price of a single glass of Bourbon, my friend Carey Jones, did me a huge favor and expertly proofread the manuscript. Marketing was by always insightful, Jade Calegory, at Jade Studios. Special thanks to Richard Hine for permission to use portions of his text. My most frequent sources were *The New York Times, Financial Times, CNN, Wall Street Journal, Washington Post, Huffington Post, Politico, Vox*, and *New York Daily News*. Thank you to the journalists and supportive staff, and brave individuals everywhere, that shine light on truth.

## ABOUT THE AUTHOR

Will Friese was raised in the suburbs of Chicago, Illinois. He graduated with a degree in engineering from Cornell University in 1988. He was done with engineering by 1990. That winter, in Colorado, while waiting tables, snowboarding, and watching CNN updates on the Gulf War, he discovered medicine as his true calling. After receiving a medical degree from the University of Pittsburgh in 1997, he moved to Phoenix, Arizona, where he practices General Surgery. He again is feeling the itch to change careers. Finance is looking good; writing is not.

OTHER WORKS BY WILLIAM FRIESE:

Made in the USA
Columbia, SC
09 September 2020